A WOMEN'S SUFFRAGE

TIME CAPSULE

ARTIFACTS of the MOVEMENT
FOR VOTING RIGHTS

by Rebecca Stanborough

Consultant:
Richard Bell, PhD
Associate Professor of History
University of Maryland, College Park

T0050832

CAPSTONE PRESS
a capstone imprint

Capstone Captivate is published by Capstone Press, an imprint of Capstone.
1710 Roe Crest Drive
North Mankato, Minnesota 56003
www.capstonepub.com

Library of Congress Cataloging-in-Publication Data is available on the Library of Congress website.
ISBN: 978-1-5435-9234-4 (library binding)
ISBN: 978-1-4966-6632-1 (paperback)
ISBN: 978-1-5435-9241-2 (eBook pdf)

Summary: Imagine opening up a time capsule to discover dinnerware, large silk banners, and a set of old pens. Together these artifacts tell the story of women's suffrage in the United States. Explore these items and more to take a closer look at the historic fight for voting rights.

Image Credits
Alamy: Alpha Stock, 34; Collection of the Smithsonian National Museum of African American History and Culture: 20; Getty Images: Buyenlarge, 28, Gado/Ken Florey Suffrage Collection, 12, 30, Jay Paull, 16; Granger: 6, 24; Library of Congress: cover (left and middle), 5, 10, 17, 18, 23, 25, 26, 27, 31, 32, 33, 35, 36, 37, 43; McClung Historical Collection: Harry T. Burn Papers, 38; National Archives and Records Administration: 41; Newscom: Picture History, 19; Seneca Falls Historical Society: 14; Shutterstock: ale-kup (background), cover and throughout, Everett Historical, cover (top right), 11, 42; Smithsonian Institution: National Museum of American History/Division of Cultural and Community Life, 9, National Museum of American History/Division of Political and Military History, 40, National Portrait Gallery, 22

Editorial Credits
Editor: Julie Gassman; Designer: Lori Bye; Media Researcher: Svetlana Zhurkin; Production Specialist: Tori Abraham

All internet sites appearing in back matter were available and accurate when this book was sent to press.

Printed in the United States of America.
PA117

Table of Contents

Words in **bold** are in the glossary.

CHAPTER 1
INTRODUCTION

When something important happens, we want to remember it. One of the ways we can do that is to save special things from that event. Artifacts such as letters, clothing, and artwork can be evidence that helps to prove what happened, show how people reacted, and remind us what was important about that moment in time. This collection of items could even be kept in a time capsule—a container of artifacts buried away for discovery in the future.

What if there were a special time capsule for each important moment in history? What if you found one of these time capsules? What might be in it?

Fact Box

The word *suffrage* means the right to vote. In the United States, the women who fought for the vote were called suffragists. While the first recorded use of the word was in 1818, it was not commonly used until after the Civil War (1861–1865).

Life was very different for women in the United States 150 years ago. The law said women were the property of their husbands and fathers, like a horse or a pair of boots. Single women could not own a house. Married women could not keep their children if their marriage ended. And women could not change these unfair laws —because they could not vote.

More than 170 years ago, women called **suffragists** began a battle for equal rights. They paraded and protested. They were mocked, beaten up, and jailed. Nevertheless, they persisted. Now imagine a time capsule dedicated to their story.

On March 3, 1913, women suffragists marched on Pennsylvania Avenue in Washington, D.C., in a huge parade to support the fight for the vote.

CHAPTER 2

BEGINNINGS

From the Time Capsule:
WAMPUM BELT

TIME CAPSULE
ARTIFACT:
WAMPUM BELT

As you open the time capsule, you notice a belt made of delicate beads. You run your fingers over smooth rows of purple and white clamshells. It is a wampum belt from the American Indian Haudenosaunee Confederacy.

In the 1840s, the first suffragists in the United States did not have to *imagine* a land where women were equal to men. It existed right in their own country.

Long before Europeans arrived in North America, one of the oldest **democracies** in the world was already thriving here, the Haudenosaunee Confederacy. Six American Indian nations—the Mohawks, the Oneidas, the Onondagas, the Cayugas, the Senecas, and, later, the Tuscaroras—joined together in what is now New York State and the provinces of Quebec and Ontario in Canada.

In Haudenosaunee societies, women are equal to men. Clan mothers choose the chiefs. They give the chosen chief a wampum belt. Although the wampum are called belts, they are not worn as clothing. Instead they are considered documents that record **treaties** and other historic moments.

If chiefs behave badly, clan mothers can take away their power. Women own land and personal property. Historically, they could declare war and work out peace treaties. And clan membership passes from mother to child. When the community needs to make decisions, *everyone* has a voice.

Early women's rights leaders lived near Haudenosaunee societies. They saw how life could be for other women.

TIME CAPSULE
ARTIFACT:
ENSLAVEMENT CHAINS

Moving the wampum belt aside, you might hear a metallic clink. Beneath the beads lies a twisted length of chain with two manacles at either end. You touch the metal edges and understand in an instant. These are the chains that kept a person enslaved. They are hard and cold.

In the 1800s, Americans were fighting two big battles. One was getting the vote for women. The other was the fight to end slavery. Many suffragists were active in both causes.

Suffragists Lucretia Mott, Susan B. Anthony, Elizabeth Cady Stanton, Lucy Stone, Matilda Gage, and many others toured the country speaking against slavery. African American leaders also fought for women's right to vote. **Abolitionist** Frederick Douglass spoke at the first Women's Rights **Convention** in 1848. And Sojourner Truth, a female minister who was once enslaved, became a champion of women's rights.

Elizabeth Cady Stanton (left) and Susan B. Anthony

Frederick
Douglass

Abolitionists and suffragists shared the same goal. They believed all people should have the same rights. The fight to end slavery taught suffragists how to organize large meetings. They learned how to protest and raise money for a cause. Later on, problems would arise between the two movements. But in the early days, they made each other stronger.

Fact Box

What is abolition? Abolition comes from the word *abolish*. When you abolish something, you end it. The 13th **Amendment** abolished slavery in 1865.

From the Time Capsule: SUFFRAGIST DINNERWARE

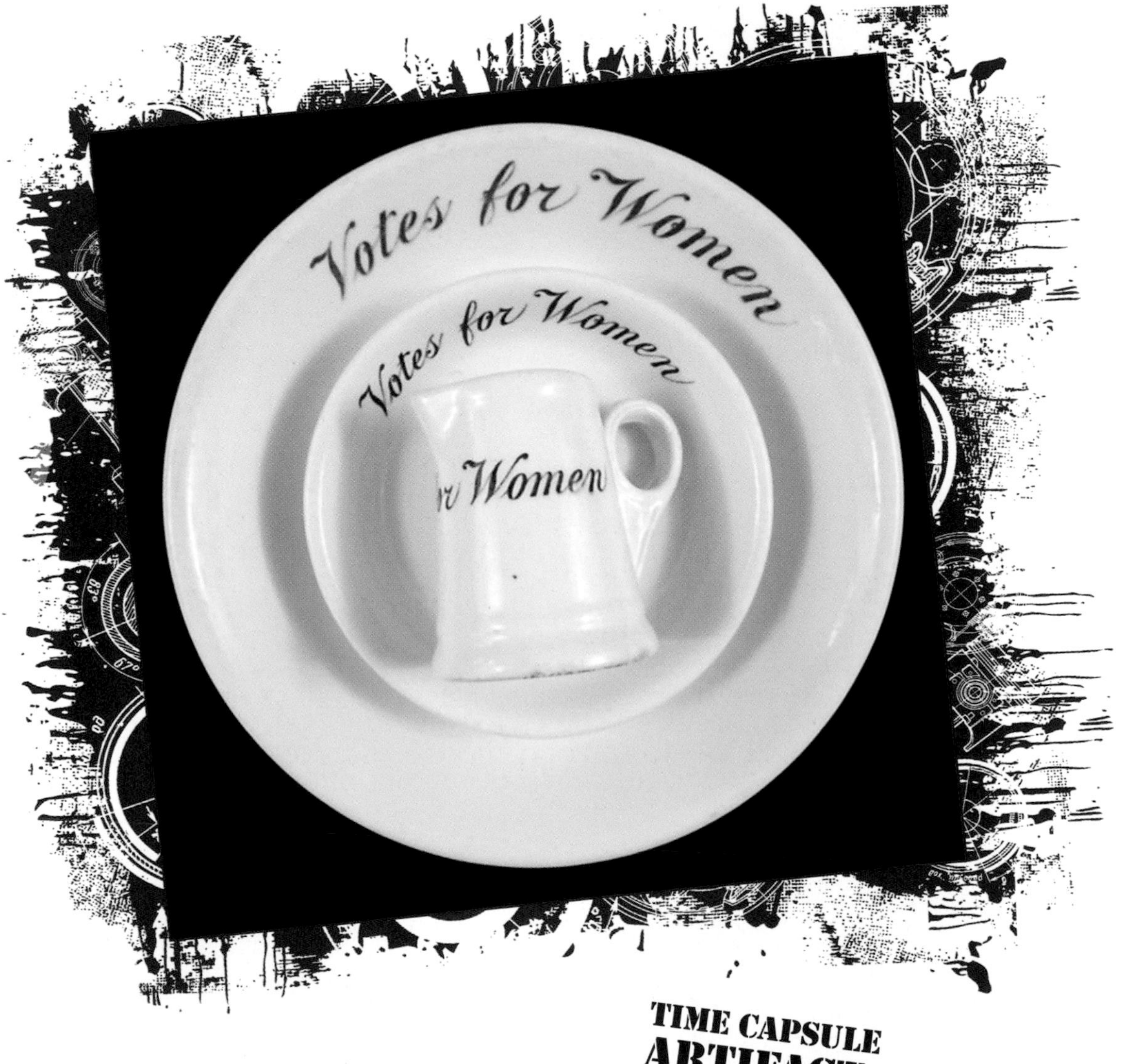

TIME CAPSULE ARTIFACT:
DINNERWARE

What else might this time capsule hold? There. Something white in the dark depths of the trunk. Gently, you lift out a blue and white plate with matching bowl and jug. *Votes for Women* is printed on each dish in an elegant script. Maddock & Sons, a British pottery company, designed this set for Alva Belmont. She hosted tea parties to raise money for the suffrage cause at her Rhode Island mansion.

Big changes often start small. For many years, female friends met in parlors and on porches to talk about their rights. These small tea gatherings might have seemed unimportant, but friendship **empowers** women. On July 9, 1848, five people—Jane Hunt, Lucretia Mott, Elizabeth Cady Stanton, Martha Wright, and Mary Ann McClintock—sat on Hunt's red velvet sofa, sipping tea. They shared their anger about the problems women faced. Two days later, Mott placed the ad in the Seneca Falls, New York, newspaper.

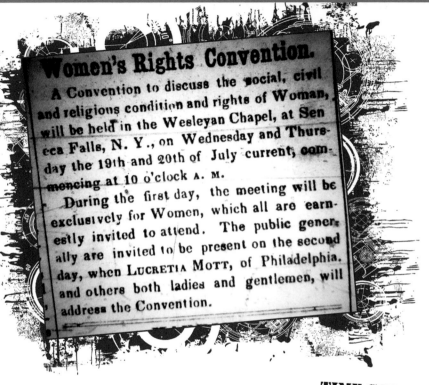

Women's Rights Convention.

A Convention to discuss the social, civil and religious condition and rights of Woman, will be held in the Wesleyan Chapel, at Seneca Falls, N. Y., on Wednesday and Thursday the 19th and 20th of July current, commencing at 10 o'clock A. M.

During the first day, the meeting will be exclusively for Women, which all are earnestly invited to attend. The public generally are invited to be present on the second day, when LUCRETIA MOTT, of Philadelphia, and others both ladies and gentlemen, will address the Convention.

TIME CAPSULE ARTIFACT:
NEWSPAPER CLIPPING

Under the weight of the fragile dishes, a scrap of paper crinkles. You pick it up and squint at the faded ink. It announced a public meeting to talk about the rights of women. This tiny newspaper clipping sparked a big change.

Lucretia Mott placed the small ad in her local newspaper, the *Seneca Falls Courier*, on July 11, 1848. When she arrived at Wesleyan Chapel on July 19, she was shocked to find more than 300 people waiting. At the two-day Seneca Falls Convention, Elizabeth Cady Stanton read her Declaration of Sentiments. It was patterned after the Declaration of Independence. In it, women demanded equal treatment. One hundred men and women signed their names to it, as the founding fathers had done to the new nation's declaration.

In the months to come, women's rights conventions took place in towns all across the United States. Then, more than 1,000 women from 11 states met at a national convention in Worcester, Massachusetts, in October 1850. From 1850 until the Civil War broke out in 1861, national conventions met every year except 1857. The fight for the vote was underway.

Fact Box

When the Civil War began, most women's rights activists stopped working for the vote. They focused on the war effort. National meetings started again after the war ended in 1865.

From the Time Capsule:
BICYCLE BELL ADVERTISEMENT

**TIME CAPSULE
ARTIFACT:**
ADVERTISEMENT

If you reach inside the trunk again, you may discover another piece of paper. This one is an ad for a bicycle bell, the kind that clamps onto a bicycle's handlebar.

In the 1890s, Americans went wild over a new piece of technology. It was called the "safety bicycle." Unlike early bikes that had a huge front wheel and a small rear wheel, this bike had wheels that were equal in size. It had a chain system that made it easy to pedal. Suddenly, women did not have to depend on men for local transportation. They could go wherever they wanted.

The sight of so many women on bikes upset some people. They were shocked to see women's ankles as they pedaled. Some even said riding a bike would make women bowlegged.

Bicycles were affordable for many women.

But the invention of the safety bicycle brought women the freedom they needed to go out and get the vote. Susan B. Anthony said, "Let me tell you what I think of bicycling. I think it has done more to **emancipate** women than anything else in the world."

From the Time Capsule:
LITHOGRAPH OF BLOOMERS

Looking into the time capsule again, you might see an illustration. In the picture, a woman stands in a garden, wearing the strangest clothes. It looks like she couldn't decide whether to wear a dress or pants—so she wore them both! Across the bottom, it is labeled "THE BLOOMER COSTUME."

Elizabeth Smith Miller, Elizabeth Cady Stanton's cousin, wanted to go out and garden. But her clothes were in the way. Like many women of the era, Miller wore a corset around her waist. Corsets were laced tightly to give women an hourglass shape. They made it hard to breathe. Miller also wore heavy layers of petticoats under her long skirt.

Amelia Bloomer, shown in what was called the "bloomer costume," wrote that the outfit was comfortable.

She was sick of it.

One day, Miller ditched the corset. She wore a skirt cut off at the knee. Underneath, she wore baggy pants that allowed her to move freely. She had seen this kind of outfit when she traveled to Europe. Miller wore the outfit when she met Amelia Bloomer, the editor of a feminist newspaper. When Bloomer wrote about Miller's outfit, her readers begged for the pattern so they could sew an outfit for themselves. The "bloomers" craze was born!

CHAPTER 4

THE DIVIDE OVER DIVERSITY

From the Time Capsule:
LIFTING AS WE CLIMB BANNER

Replacing the bloomers picture, your hand might brush across something silky. If you lift it into the light, you'll be able to read its golden letters: *LIFTING AS WE CLIMB*. The banner's satiny fringe dances over your fingertips. The Oklahoma Federation of Colored Women's Clubs created this banner around 1924 in its fight to improve their life in the black community. It represents the role that black Americans played in the fight for suffrage.

TIME CAPSULE ARTIFACT:
SILK BANNER

President Abraham Lincoln signed the **Emancipation Proclamation** on January 1, 1863. It freed enslaved people in the southern states. Activists wanted to keep fighting for equal rights for black Americans. Some thought it would be easier to get the vote for black American men than it would be to get votes for all women.

Elizabeth Cady Stanton, Susan B. Anthony, and others were furious. How could people focus on a black man's right to vote when white women still could not?

This conflict exposed deep **racism** in the movement. African American women had known the racism was there all along. Few black women held leadership roles in the women's suffrage movement. When there were public meetings, African American women were rarely asked to speak. And they were sometimes excluded from suffrage meetings in the southern states.

But racism did not keep African American women from fighting for the vote. Black women's clubs worked to empower women. Ida B. Wells-Barnett formed the Alpha Suffrage Club in Chicago in 1913. She was an important journalist who dared to report on the racist treatment of black Americans. Historians say the Alpha Suffrage Club was one of the most important suffrage groups in the United States.

Ida B. Wells-Barnett

Frances E.W. Harper

Mary Church Terrell, Josephine St. Pierre Ruffin, and Charlotte Forten Grimké founded the National Association of Colored Women (NACW). It united many U.S. black women's clubs in the fight for votes. Frances E.W. Harper, a poet and teacher, worked tirelessly for the vote. She helped found the American Woman Suffrage Association (AWSA). In an 1873 speech, Harper said, "As much as white women need the ballot, colored women need it more."

Views on race were not the only issues that separated suffragists. They also disagreed about the best way to get the vote.

Elizabeth Cady Stanton and Susan B. Anthony formed the National Woman Suffrage Association (NWSA) to press for a national amendment to the U.S. Constitution to grant women the right to vote. Lucy Stone and Julia Ward Howe led the formation of the AWSA to get the vote state by state. However, in 1890 these two organizations joined forces.

NWSA members met with members of the U.S. Congress.

CHAPTER 5

PARADES AND PROTESTS

From the Time Capsule:
SUFFRAGE PARADE PROGRAM

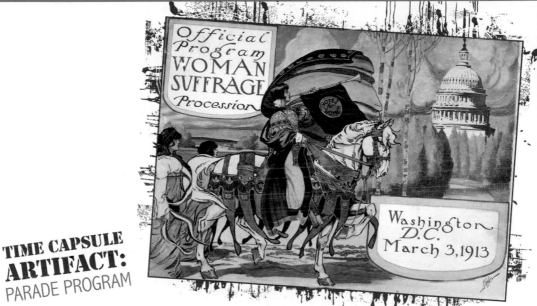

TIME CAPSULE ARTIFACT:
PARADE PROGRAM

Peering back into the time capsule, perhaps you discover a parade program printed on thick paper. On its cover a proud woman sits astride a white horse. You can almost hear that horse's spirited whinny. You imagine what it would have been like, watching that parade pass by. You might have cheered on the women as they marched past, their banners flapping in the chilly March breeze.

Alice Paul

Some women grew frustrated with the slow change. They decided to take a more radical approach. Led by Alice Paul and Lucy Burns, a new group of young activists used daring tactics to draw attention to the cause. Paul organized a huge march on Washington, D.C., on March 3, 1913, the day before Woodrow Wilson would be sworn in as U.S. president.

The parade was led by lawyer Inez Milholland. She was dressed in white and seated on a white horse. The parade included 5,000 women, nine bands, and at least 20 floats.

Inez Milholland worked for many causes, including prison reform.

Two years later, in 1915, another parade took place in New York City. Once again, marchers wore white. They draped themselves in cloth banners that read *Votes for Women.* The parade drew somewhere between 25,000 to 60,000 marchers. Marches like these took place all over the nation.

Red-Lipped Ladies

When women took to the streets of New York City to call for the vote during a 1912 march, they shouted through bold red lips. Makeup maven Elizabeth Arden had supplied lipstick in the same shade as the front door of her Fifth Avenue spa. In 2018, the company released a bright red lipstick called "March On!"

CHAPTER 6
BACKLASH

From the Time Capsule:
ANTI-SUFFRAGE POSTCARD

TIME CAPSULE
ARTIFACT:
POSTCARD

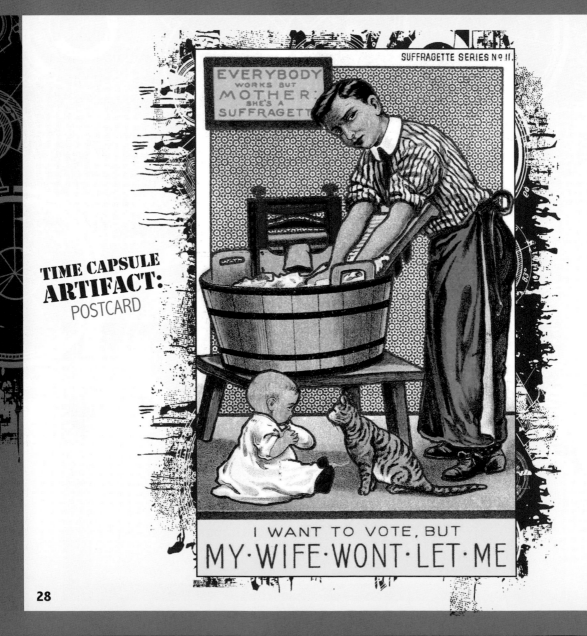

There is more to discover inside the time capsule. Reaching deep inside, your fingertips may find a stack of postcards. You take one from the top. Its negative tone might surprise you. You may wonder why anyone would want to keep women from voting. These postcards show you that people feared women with power.

The fight for the vote met with fierce **opposition**. There were plenty of men and even some women who thought that if women got the vote, the "natural order" of the world would flip upside down. They tried to make everyone afraid of what would happen if women could vote.

Newspaper cartoons suggested that voting would take away men's power. Families would be ruined. "Antis"—those who were anti-suffrage—also sent out **propaganda** postcards. These postcards made suffragists look ugly and angry. They made men look like housewives.

WHAT I WOULD DO WITH THE SUFFRAGISTS.

56 lbs

Women in the United Kingdom also fought for suffrage around the same time. A British anti-suffrage postcard from 1900 encouraged violence against suffragists.

Some postcards even threatened violence to try to stop women from voting. Unfortunately, violence against suffragists was not just postcard propaganda. When women marched, young men and boys shouted at them. Men kicked them and tore off their sashes. Police officers stood by and did nothing. When at last the police would step in, they arrested the women!

The Allender Girls

The suffragists fought back with their own brand of propaganda. Artist Nina Allender drew more than 200 cartoons for suffragist newspapers. Her cartoons challenged the idea that suffragists were "mannish." She presented suffragists as stylish, young, *and* serious about equal rights. The women in her cartoons were known as "Allender Girls."

Nina Allender was the main artist for Alice Paul's publication, *The Suffragist*.

CHAPTER 7
SUFFERING FOR THE CAUSE

From the Time Capsule:
CLOTH PROTEST BANNER

TIME CAPSULE
ARTIFACT:
PROTEST BANNER

MR. PRESIDENT HOW LONG MUST WOMEN WAIT FOR LIBERTY

At first, you could mistake the next artifact for a bedsheet. But as you unfold it, you might realize that this long piece of white cloth did more to wake people up than to put them to sleep.

Alice Paul, Lucy Burns, and the National Woman's Party refused to quietly wait for the vote. Instead, they got out their needles and sewed. They made big banners with loud voting messages on them. Then they **picketed** in front of the White House, starting in 1917.

Alice Paul emerged from the National Woman's Party headquarters in Washington, D.C., with a large protest banner.

TIME CAPSULE ARTIFACT:
SILVER PIN

Placing the white banner back in the capsule, you might notice a small red box. Inside is a silver pin that looks like the door of an old jail cell. A heart-shaped lock dangles from a tiny, delicate chain. It is a badge of honor, given to recognize the bravery of suffragists who went to jail for their protests.

Suffragists protested the treatment of Alice Paul and other activists jailed at the Occoquan Workhouse.

In June 1917, police arrested some of the picketers and threw them into jail at the Occoquan Workhouse. Some women were injured because of how harshly police officers treated them. At first, President Wilson pardoned the women. But when they continued to protest, they were jailed again and again. In all, about 200 women were sent to jail for demanding the vote.

In the Occoquan prison, conditions were terrible. It was teeming with rats. The food was full of maggots. And many other prisoners had contagious sicknesses. To protest their treatment, some of the women went on a hunger strike. They refused to eat while they were in prison. The guards put tubes down their throats and forced milk into their stomachs.

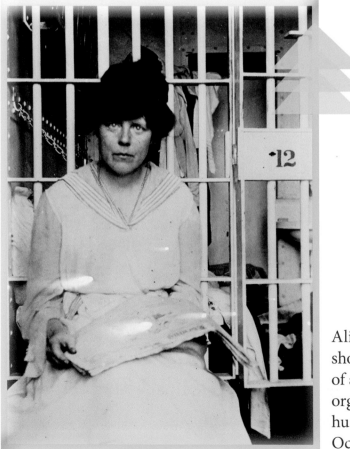

Alice Paul, shown in front of a prison cell, organized the hunger strike at Occoquan.

Exterior of cell blocks at the Occoquan Workhouse

The women who won the vote sacrificed their freedom, their reputations, and their health for their cause. When the prison doors slammed and the guards left them alone in their cells, not one of them knew for sure if their courage would make any difference.

When the "jailbirds" were finally released for good, they received these pins.

From the Time Capsule:
LETTER FROM HOME

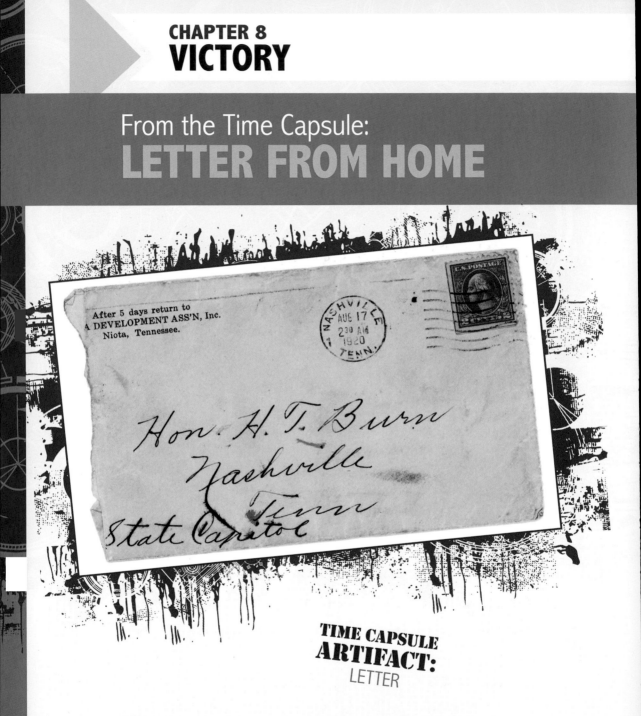

After 5 days return to
A DEVELOPMENT ASS'N, Inc.
Niota, Tennessee.

NASHVILLE
AUG 17
2 30 AM
1920
TENN.

Hon. H. T. Burn
Nashville
Tenn
State Capitol

TIME CAPSULE
ARTIFACT:
LETTER

There is one last piece of paper in the antique travel trunk. It is a letter, yellow with age.

Suffragists kept putting pressure on President Wilson and Congress. Finally, their bold tactics paid off. On June 4, 1919, the 19th Amendment passed Congress. But in order to become the law of the land, the amendment would have to be approved, or **ratified,** by 36 states. Tennessee was the last state needed. It was going to be tight. The vote for suffrage came down to one young man: Harry T. Burn. He had just been elected to Tennessee's state legislature. Burn had planned to vote no. But then he got a letter that turned his vote around.

The letter was from his mother, Febb E. Burn. She wrote:

"Dear Son, . . . Hurrah and vote for Suffrage and don't keep them in doubt. . . . I've been waiting to see how you stood but have not seen any thing yet. . . . Don't forget to be a good boy, and help Mrs. 'Thomas Catt' with her 'Rats.' Is she the one that put rat in ratification, Ha! ... With lots of love, Mama."

After Harry read his mother's words, he voted yes. The 19th Amendment was law.

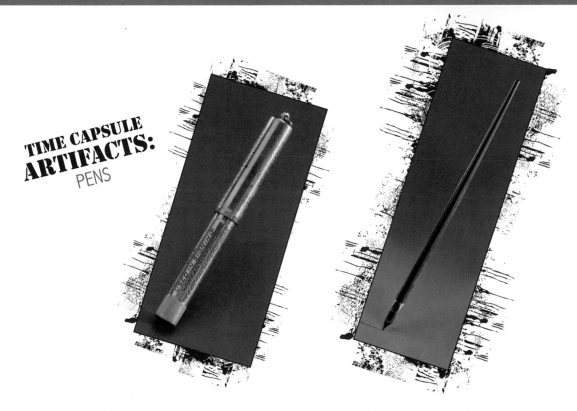

TIME CAPSULE
ARTIFACTS:
PENS

The final items in our time capsule are valuable for their historical significance. In June 1919, Vice President Thomas Marshall and Speaker of the House Frederick Gillett signed a resolution recommending the 19th Amendment. They used the golden pen. U.S. Secretary of State Bainbridge Colby used the wooden pen to sign the ratification almost a year later, giving women the vote.

The gleaming pen might give you an unexpected jolt of joy—because this is the pen that set the 19th Amendment in motion. If you were to try and scribble your name with one of these pens, as if you were signing the amendment yourself, you would discover that the ink has long since dried. That's OK. These pens served a noble purpose, and their work is done. They proclaimed to the whole nation that women have the right to vote.

Official 19th Amendment document signed by Marshall and Gillett

H. J. Res. 1.

Sixty-sixth Congress of the United States of America;

At the First Session,

Begun and held at the City of Washington on Monday, the nineteenth day of May, one thousand nine hundred and nineteen.

JOINT RESOLUTION

Proposing an amendment to the Constitution extending the right of suffrage to women.

Resolved by the Senate and House of Representatives of the United States of America in Congress assembled (two-thirds of each House concurring therein), That the following article is proposed as an amendment to the Constitution, which shall be valid to all intents and purposes as part of the Constitution when ratified by the legislatures of three-fourths of the several States.

"ARTICLE ———

"The right of citizens of the United States to vote shall not be denied or abridged by the United States or by any State on account of sex.

"Congress shall have power to enforce this article by appropriate legislation."

F. H. Gillett
Speaker of the House of Representatives.

Thos. R. Marshall
Vice President of the United States and President of the Senate.

The 1920 election was the first time American women voted for U.S. president.

On August 18, 1920, women finally won the vote. Seventy-two years had passed since the Seneca Falls Convention. Only one of the people who signed the Declaration of Sentiments lived to see the day when women could vote. Her name was Charlotte Woodward Pierce.

Charlotte Woodward Pierce

There is one more artifact that would make a great addition to this historical collection. Reader, when you are old enough to vote, a poll worker might give you a sticker that says, *I Voted*. The souvenir you collect when you cast your first vote belongs right here, along with the photos, postcards, and banners created by your suffragist sisters.

More About the Artifacts

Wampum Belt

This belt was crafted in the early 19th century near the eastern coast of North America. Different shell patterns depicted different agreements. Wampum belts might be used to show treaties between tribes. They might also show marriage agreements or religious events, in addition to the nomination of chiefs.

Enslavement Chains

This pair of enslavement shackles is part of the collection at the Smithsonian National Museum of American History in Washington, D.C. They were forged in Puerto Rico in the 1800s.

Suffragist Dinnerware

This dinnerware collection, which included several other pieces, was created by Maddock & Sons in 1914 for Alva Belmont, a wealthy socialite who supported women's suffrage. Belmont sold pieces of the dinnerware as a fundraiser to support women's suffrage.

Newspaper Announcement

Lucretia Mott placed this announcement in the *Seneca Falls Courier* before the first Women's Rights Convention in Seneca Falls, New York. A similar announcement ran in *The North Star*, the newspaper published by Frederick Douglass.

Bicycle Bell Advertisement

Bicycle bells were invented by John Dedicoat around 1887, well into the suffrage movement. The bell pictured in this advertisement was made by the New Departure Bell Company in Bristol, Connecticut. The company started out making doorbells. When bicycle sales took off, New Departure began making clamp-on bells for handlebars.

Lithograph of Bloomers

This lithograph was published in 1851 in New York by Currier and Ives, a successful American printmaking firm. Printing lithographic prints was a fast process, so they could publish many of them and at an affordable price to the buyers.

LIFTING AS WE CLIMB Banner

The Oklahoma Federation of Colored Women's Clubs banner is made of silk and measures 37¼ inches (95 centimeters) long and 31½ inches (80 cm) wide. The banner is housed in the Smithsonian National Museum of African American History and Culture in Washington, D.C.

Suffrage Parade Program

This official program was edited by Harriet Brown, a reporter, writer, and editor. In the program, Brown published detailed information about the women who put together the 1913 march. In that era, the work of women often went unnoticed. Seeing the accomplishments of so many suffragists must have inspired the women who witnessed the parade.

Anti-Suffrage Postcard

Dozens of postcards like these played on people's fears. Some showed women wearing men's clothing. Many showed women talking, smoking, and drinking with their friends while their husbands did housework. These cartoons stoked the fear that letting women vote would destroy society's gender norms.

Cloth Protest Banner

Alice Paul had a gift for attracting media attention. As one of the founders of the National Woman's Party, she knew it was important to keep the voting issue in the news. Banners with bold messages would do the trick. The banners outraged President Woodrow Wilson. No one had ever picketed in front of the White House before—and the banners embarrassed him.

Silver Suffragist Pin

Suffragists gave out these pins to any woman who had been imprisoned for her role in picketing the White House. The "Jailed for Freedom" pins were designed by Nina Allender. Historians think about 200 of these pins were made.

Letter from Home

Febb E. Burn knew her son Harry was worried about being re-elected. In Harry's district, people were sharply divided over whether women should have the vote. Febb Burn knew her son would be torn about how to vote. So she stepped out onto the porch on her Tennessee farm, picked up her pen, and dashed off a seven-page letter. And Harry turned out to be a very good boy indeed.

Historical Pens

Both of these pens played a part in getting women the vote. In June 1919, the vice president and the Speaker of the House signed a joint resolution that recommended a 19th Amendment allowing women to vote. To amend the U.S. Constitution, at least 36 states had to ratify the amendment. Once the 36th state voted yes in August 1920, the second pen was used to sign the amendment into law. Both pens are part of the Smithsonian National Museum of American History.

Glossary

abolitionist (ab-uh-LISH-uh-nist)—a person who worked to end slavery

amendment (uh-MEND-muhnt)—a formal change made to a law or legal document, such as the U.S. Constitution

convention (kuhn-VEN-shuhn)—a large gathering of people who have the same interests

democracy (di-MAH-kruh-see)—a form of government in which citizens can choose their leaders

emancipate (i-MAN-si-payt)—to free someone from the control of another

Emancipation Proclamation (i-MAN-si-pay-shuhn prok-luh-MAY-shuhn)—a document signed by President Abraham Lincoln during the Civil War, which freed the slaves in areas under Confederate control

empower (em-POW-er)—to give authority or legal power

opposition (op-uh-ZISH-uhn)—the people fighting against something

picket (PIK-it)—to stand in a public place to spread your message

propaganda (prop-ah-GAN-da)—information spread to try and influence the thinking of people; often not completely true or fair

racism (RAY-si-zuhm)—the belief that one race is better than another

ratify (RAT-uh-fye)—formally approve

suffragist (SUHF-rih-jist)—a person who supports extending voting rights, especially to women

treaty (TREE-tee)—an official agreement between two or more groups or countries

Read More

Bartoletti, Susan Campbell. *How Women Won the Vote: Alice Paul, Lucy Burns, and Their Big Idea*. New York: Harper Collins, 2020.

Gillibrand, Kirsten. *Bold & Brave: Ten Heroes Who Won Women the Right to Vote*. New York: Alfred A. Knopf, 2018.

Sohn, Emily. *National Woman's Party Fight for Suffrage*. North Mankato, MN: Capstone, 2021.

Internet Sites

African American Reformers
www.womenshistory.org/resources/general/african-american-reformers

Lucretia Mott: An Early Voice for Equality
www.womenshistory.org/sites/default/files/document/2018-08/Full%20Color%20Comic%20PDF.pdf

Woman's Suffrage History Timeline
www.nps.gov/wori/learn/historyculture/womens-suffrage-history-timeline.htm

Index